T0195980

To order additional copies of this book, contact:
Xlibris
844-714-8691
www.Xlibris.com
Orders@Xlibris.com

ISBN: Softcover   978-1-6641-5320-2
       EBook   978-1-6641-5321-9

Print information available on the last page

Rev. date: 01/19/2021

This is the story of Haven and the lessons she learns that ultimately lead her to be Happy Haven.

Sharing

One time, Haven was invited to a friend's birthday party. She was excited to go. There would be lots of fun and tons of cake.

Some of Haven's siblings—Cooper, Ella, Lincoln, and Abigail—wished they could have cake.

What should Haven do?

Sharing is when we give what we have to someone else.

Haven loves her family and wants her siblings to enjoy some cake too. She brought home extra cake just for her family.

Haven shared, and she was happy.

Thoughtful

Reading Books to Siblings

Haven's younger sisters Ella and Abigail and her brother Lincoln cannot read yet, but they love to look at the pictures. Many nights, after getting ready for bed, Haven notices them flipping through the pages of different books.

What should Haven do?

To be thoughtful is to recognize the needs of others and try to help them.

Haven chose to sit down and read books to Ella, Lincoln, and Abigail. They were so happy. She cared about her family. She was thoughtful, and she was happy.

Friend's

Being a Friend to Someone Lonely at School

Haven loves school and loves playing with her friends.

One day at recess, there was a girl named Kaitlyn who was sitting all alone. She looked sad and lonely.

What should Haven do?

A friend is someone that cares for you and wants you to be happy.

Haven wanted Kaitlyn to be happy, so she chose to sit beside her and play with her.

Kaitlyn was not alone anymore. Haven was her friend and she was happy.

Diligence

Haven Diligently Practicing Piano

Haven loves to sing and play the piano. Her mom told her she needed to practice piano every day.

One day, Haven had been playing freeze tag with her sister Ella and friends Maggie and Lottie.

Haven was super tired and just wanted to go to sleep.

What should she do?

Being diligent means working hard at something even when it's tough.

Even though Haven was tired, she knew she should practice piano every day. Haven was diligent. Haven was happy.

Printed in the United States
By Bookmasters